THE PEOPLE

The
Articles of Confederation

by Renée C. Rebman

Content Adviser: Melodie Andrews, Ph.D.,
Associate Professor of Early American and Women's History,
Minnesota State University, Mankato

Reading Adviser: Rosemary Palmer, Ph.D.,
Department of Literacy, College of Education,
Boise State University

COMPASS POINT BOOKS
MINNEAPOLIS, MINNESOTA

Compass Point Books
3109 West 50th Street, #115
Minneapolis, MN 55410

Visit Compass Point Books on the Internet at *www.compasspointbooks.com*
or e-mail your request to *custserv@compasspointbooks.com*

On the cover: Title page of the first printed copy of the Articles of Confederation, 1777

Photographs ©: The Granger Collection, New York, cover, 7, 9, 17, 34; Prints Old and Rare, back
cover (far left); Library of Congress, back cover; North Wind Picture Archives, 5, 24, 26, 29, 37;
Stock Montage/Getty Images, 11; MPI/Getty Images, 12, 21; U.S. Capitol Historical Society/
Declaration of Independence by John Trumbull, 14; National Portrait Gallery, Smithsonian
Institution/Art Resource, N.Y., 23; Burstein Collection/Corbis, 31; Bettmann/Corbis, 32, 38;
Bristol City Museum and Art Gallery, UK/The Bridgeman Art Library, 41.

Editor: Nick Healy
Page Production: The Design Lab
Photo Researcher: Svetlana Zhurkin
Cartographer: XNR Productions, Inc.
Library Consultant: Kathleen Baxter

Creative Director: Keith Griffin
Editorial Director: Carol Jones
Managing Editor: Catherine Neitge

Library of Congress Cataloging-in-Publication Data
Rebman, Renée C., 1961–
  The Articles of Confederation / by Renee C. Rebman.
      p. cm. — (We the people)
  Includes bibliographical references and index.
  ISBN 0-7565-1627-7 (hardcover)
  1. United States. Articles of Confederation—Juvenile literature. 2. Constitutional history—
United States—Sources—Juvenile literature. 3. United States—Politics and government—1775–
1783—Juvenile literature. I. Title. II. We the people (Series) (Compass Point Books)
  KF4508.R43 2006
  342.7302'9—dc22   2005025065

TABLE OF CONTENTS

FORMING A NEW NATION

A sweltering heat gripped the city of Philadelphia during the summer of 1776. The Second Continental Congress gathered at the Pennsylvania State House to make an important decision. Should the 13 colonies break away from Britain and declare independence?

Some of the delegates—people sent to represent each of the colonies—supported the call for independence, while others did not. The men debated for more than a month as they worked toward agreement on the best course for their homeland.

At the time, the American Revolution was under way. War had broken out in April 1775. Parliament, the governing body of England, forced the colonists to obey English laws. Parliament also made the colonists pay many taxes, which the Americans had no power and no vote in creating. Many colonists believed this was unfair, and they hoped their revolt would force Parliament to change. But

4

after more than a year of fighting, Parliament showed no sign of budging. With no hope of change, many colonial citizens wanted to break away from England entirely. The call for independence became stronger with each passing day. At the convention, delegates struggled with what would become a historic decision.

On June 7, 1776, a Virginian named Richard Henry Lee offered a formal resolution—or, made a motion—that

American soldiers overwhelm a British position during the Revolutionary War.

two important documents be drafted. He asked that a declaration of independence be prepared and that Congress form "a plan for confederation." Lee wanted the colonies to be unified, and he believed they needed an organized plan in place if they were to break from England. Lee's resolution was a turning point in the discussions.

Four days later, members of Congress responded. They appointed committees to draft the two documents. One document would declare independence. It became the famous Declaration of Independence. The other document was called the Articles of Confederation. It would set the structure and define the powers of the new government.

John Dickinson, a delegate from Delaware, would bear the responsibility for writing the first draft of the Articles of Confederation. He seemed a natural choice for the job. In the 1760s, he had written newspaper articles that explained the colonists' opposition to British taxes. The articles were then published together as a pamphlet. His work won him the nickname "Penman of the Revolution."

The idea of a formal plan to unite the colonies was not new. Benjamin Franklin had presented such a plan a year earlier. At the time, there was no move toward independence. The colonists mostly wanted to get Parliament's attention and to bring about changes in British policy. Franklin's idea of a constitution was considered unneces-

John Dickinson

sary. By 1776, that was no longer the case. Breaking away from the rule of King George III meant the colonists would have to govern themselves.

While the Revolutionary War continued to rage, a new chapter in history began. The 13 colonies became the United States of America. The Founding Fathers intended to build a new nation, with the Articles of Confederation as its foundation.

BRITISH RULE

For many years, colonists were proud to be British citizens. They trusted and loved their mother country. They felt Parliament was looking out for their best interests. After the French and Indian War ended in 1763, England started keeping a closer eye on the colonists and maintained troops in North America to protect the new territory won in the war. The colonies were prospering, and Parliament levied taxes on the colonists, as it did on people in England.

In 1765, Parliament passed the Stamp Act, which called for a new tax on colonists. Money raised by the tax was supposed to pay for British army troops stationed in America. The new tax meant an additional charge on all paper goods, including newspapers, almanacs, marriage licenses, and legal documents such as deeds and mortgages. The tax was immediately unpopular with Americans. Protest against the Stamp Act was strong. Angry colonists

8

destroyed property, threatened violence, and even tarred and feathered officials who supported the tax.

Delegates from nine of the colonies gathered in New York City late in 1765 to protest the tax. This gathering was called the Stamp Act Congress. Delegates called the Stamp Act "taxation without representation." And without representation in Parliament, they felt any tax was unfair.

Eventually the British Parliament repealed the Stamp Act, but that would not end the troubles in America. Instead of taxes on paper products,

Officials who enforced the Stamp Act were tarred and feathered during a 1765 demonstration.

9

Parliament imposed a variety of new taxes. The tension over taxes only grew. Colonists who had once been supportive of England became resentful.

British officials believed England had a long and proud history of fairness to citizens. In fact, one of the first political documents to address and guarantee the basic rights of private citizens had been created in England hundreds of years earlier. That famous document was the Magna Carta, which King John signed in 1215. Its ideas were studied and admired for centuries.

On the matter of taxation, the Magna Carta was straightforward. It clearly stated taxes should be created only by consent of the people. The document said, "No scutage (a type of tax) or aid should be imposed in our realm unless by the common counsel of the realm."

In the 1700s, members of Parliament believed they were governing by consent of the people, or "common counsel," even though not by directly elected representation. Lawmakers believed the colonies belonged to England, so

Parliament was entitled—even obligated—to govern the colonies.

In 1690, English philosopher John Locke had challenged such ideas. Locke said people had a right to life, liberty, and property. He believed that people had a right to rebel. He felt they should overthrow leaders and change government if necessary.

John Locke

Locke's startling new philosophy influenced thinking in the colonies.

The Founding Fathers embraced Locke's thinking. His ideas gave them the courage to support the movement toward independence. The Articles of Confederation would take shape around key ideas expressed by Locke and in the Magna Carta, and the days of British rule in the colonies would soon end.

11

DRAFTING THE DOCUMENT

John Dickinson had a difficult and important task. After being chosen by members of the Second Continental Congress to draft the Articles of Confederation, Dickinson had to combine the best principles and ideas into a document that would serve the 13 colonies well. He had many opinions and viewpoints to consider.

John Dickinson was nicknamed "Penman of the Revolution."

Dickinson wrote his draft in separate sections. Each section concerned a specific topic. Dickinson used many of Benjamin Franklin's ideas. He suggested Congress take money from each state and keep it in a treasury. He also suggested Congress should have control over war matters. Like Franklin, he wanted the United States to establish its own post office.

Unlike Franklin, he felt each state

should have one vote regardless of its size or population. Franklin wanted states with more people living in them to have more votes in Congress.

The delegates found some problems with the draft. The 13 colonies (soon to become states) wanted to keep their own rights and powers, especially when it came to taxation. They did not want to be overpowered by a strong central government. This feeling was understandable, considering how they had suffered under the rule of King George.

Yet it was also important that they form a strong union. Delegates argued over how much power Congress should have. One delegate, James Wilson, argued that Congress should represent all people, not the states. He wanted Congress to protect the rights of individual citizens. He didn't want the states to have strong power or a lot of control. He worried it would divide the country. In his autobiography, Thomas Jefferson later recalled that Wilson's belief was that "we are not so many states, we are one large state." For the Second Continental Congress, finding a

13

balance of power seemed for a time to be impossible.

At the same time Jefferson was writing the Declaration of Independence, Dickinson worked nonstop to finish his draft. It was read to the Congress on July 12, 1776, eight days after the Declaration was adopted. Eighty copies of Dickinson's document were printed and distributed to delegates for consideration. The delegates and the printers were sworn to secrecy as to its contents.

On July 22, discussions began about possible changes

Colonial leaders voted to accept the Declaration of Independence on July 4, 1776.

to the Articles. Delegates wanted to be very specific about what the government could and could not do. They wrote and rewrote dozens of pages. After 16 days of debate, spread out over nearly a month, delegates agreed upon a complete form of the Articles of Confederation, which would be presented to the states for ratification. The document consisted of 13 sections, which were largely devoted to placing limits on the new government.

The states retained much of their individual power and independence. They would have their own state laws and taxes. Article Two affirmed, "Each state retains its sovereignty, freedom and independence, and every power, jurisdiction and right, which is not by this confederation expressly delegated to the United States, in Congress assembled." In other words, Congress would only have powers that were specifically given to it. Individual states would remain in control of all other affairs within their borders. As Dickinson wanted, each state had one vote in Congress, regardless of its size or population.

The Articles did not call for a single official—a president—to lead the country. A president of Congress would be in charge of meetings, but he had no real power. When Congress was not in session, a committee was in charge. Representatives from each state were appointed to the committee.

Congress could make no changes to the Articles of Confederation without a unanimous vote. This meant each delegate from every state had to agree to an amendment before it would pass.

The Articles did not provide a system of federal courts, although it gave Congress the power to appoint a court for crimes committed at sea. The federal government could not interfere with state laws and was powerless to settle disputes, except as a last resort in disagreements between states over boundaries or other issues. Most arguments—such as ones over land or over fugitive criminals or escaped slaves who fled across state borders—would be settled by the states involved. Congress had no

16

power over interstate trade. The exchange of goods, such as cotton or tobacco, between the states was common. The states would be left to impose restrictions and collect taxes themselves.

In many ways, Congress was at the mercy of the states. It could only request taxes from the states based on their population, as Congress did throughout the war. Congress had no means of forcing states to pay. Also, it could not draft troops but depended on the states to supply them voluntarily. The new country was at war, fighting to win its freedom from British rule,

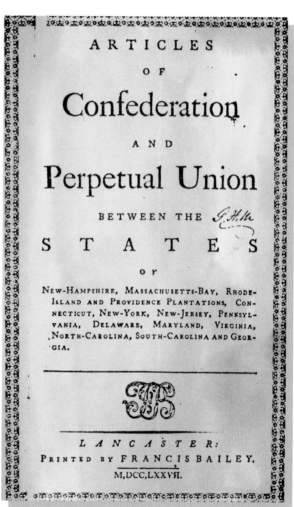

The title page of the first printed copy of the Articles of Confederation

The 13 colonies that formed the United States stretched along the Atlantic coast.

but the federal government had no guaranteed supply of money or soldiers. This would prove to be a serious problem.

The Founding Fathers began using the Articles of Confederation to guide the new nation, but the document had to be officially accepted by the states. Each state had to vote to ratify, or approve, the Articles. It was a long, slow process.

By 1779, Maryland was the only state that would not ratify the Articles. The settling of the Western frontier— then the area just beyond the Appalachian Mountains—was the last remaining problem. Congress had no power to set boundaries on new states. Existing states could simply claim newly settled land on the frontier. Virginia, for example, claimed a large swath of land beyond the Appalachians. Maryland wanted Congress to form new states in the region, rather than allowing existing states to snatch up the land.

In October 1780, Congress yielded to Maryland's wishes and resolved that the land be formed into "republican states, which shall become members of the federal union." With that matter settled, Maryland voted to ratify, and in 1781, the Articles of Confederation became the nation's first federal system of government.

THE NEWBURGH CONSPIRACY

The newly formed United States faced many difficult problems. The most pressing one was how to finance the ongoing war against Britain. Under the Articles of Confederation, the federal government depended upon cooperation from the states. Many states, however, withheld tax money and troops.

The Continental Army fighting against Britain lacked food and supplies. Many soldiers had no coats, and those without shoes marched with rags wrapped around their feet. Practically starving, they ate "fire cakes," a mixture of flour and water fried on a griddle. This was often their only meal. Soldiers chanted, "We want meat," but there was no meat available.

Commanding officers were owed back pay. They wanted the money promised to them. Also, the federal government guaranteed officers a pension, which is money paid to people who have retired, once the war ended. But

Soldiers, who were often short on food and supplies, built shelters for the winter.

Congress had no way to pay pensions. It had also promised to give soldiers land after the war. It didn't seem possible for Congress to keep any of these promises. Both the soldiers and leaders were unhappy.

One man decided he had the answer to the problem. Robert Morris, a prominent Philadelphia merchant, was the superintendent of finance for the United States. He established a national bank. He also created a plan to improve the nation's economy.

At the time, many of the states printed their own money. Currency used in one state might be worthless in another. People sometimes refused to take others' money, so citizens were unable to buy the things they wanted. Businesses suffered, and debts went unpaid. A single currency would eliminate problems. Morris wanted his bank to issue the money that all states would use.

Morris asked Congress to levy a new tax on imports in order to raise funds for his bank. An amendment to create the tax was presented in Congress, but the delegate from Rhode Island refused to support it. Because a unanimous vote was required, the amendment failed.

Morris grew angry. He wanted to show people how weak the government was without money. He wanted to frighten the states into cooperating. So he became involved in a secret plot that posed a threat to the federal government, which was still new and trying to establish stability.

Morris and other leaders who shared his frustrations began planning a military coup. They hoped to launch a surprise attack. When faced with angry troops, states would be unable to defend themselves. They would also find they could not depend on the federal government to help.

General George Washington's men were spending the winter encamped along the Hudson River in Newburgh, New York. They were exhausted and short on food and supplies. Many soldiers were sick, and morale was low. Several of Washington's officers supported the plot against the government. Then Washington

Robert Morris

discovered some of his officers were meeting and planning the attack. He confronted the officers and stopped the coup. What would later be called the Newburgh Conspiracy came to a quick end.

Morris had proposed an extreme and violent action to point out a weakness in the Articles of Confederation. It was apparent that the Articles were imperfect, but they were still effective. Under the Articles, the government kept the new nation going even during difficult war times.

The fighting between British and American forces ended after six years of bloodshed. In 1781, British General Charles Cornwallis surrendered to General Washington at Yorktown, Virginia. Two years later, Congress finally reached an agreement with Parliament. On September 3, 1783, the Treaty of Paris was signed. With the treaty, England and Parliament formally recognized the independence of the United States.

British General Cornwallis surrendered to end fighting in the Revolutionary War.

WESTWARD EXPANSION

With the Revolutionary War over, the push to settle the West was strong. Pioneers in growing numbers traveled west into land not occupied by other whites. This created a whole set of problems for the new government, which had to decide how new territory would be settled and ruled.

In the newly independent United States, people continued going west as they had before and during the war. In fact, the number of settlers only increased as pioneers left the newly formed 13 states, traveled through the mountains, and arrived in the Ohio and Kentucky territories and other lands in the area. Many people even traveled across the Mississippi River to faraway Western regions. They faced bad weather, Indian attacks, and other hardships.

American Indian tribes lost their land to the white settlers, who ignored land claims and treaties that existed to protect Indian lands. When settlements were built on Indian land, the native people moved to new wilderness

Americans began settling the frontier in growing numbers after the Revolution.

territories in order to survive.

Under the Articles of Confederation, new states formed as the lands were settled. Congress passed three major ordinances to govern the process. The Ordinance of 1784 addressed statehood. Thomas Jefferson, serving as a congressman from the state of Virginia, proposed that Western territories would self-govern until their populations equaled that of the existing state with the smallest population. When that happened, the territory would achieve full statehood.

The Land Ordinance of 1785 outlined land surveys in much of the Northwest, an area undergoing development.

This area would later become the states of Indiana, Illinois, Michigan, Wisconsin, and Minnesota. The ordinance set up townships of 6 square miles (15.6 square kilometers). Each township was divided into sections of 1 square mile (2.6 square km), or 640 acres (256 hectares). Townships included land set aside for schools and for war veterans. The government auctioned the land for $640 per section, or $1 per acre. This was an expensive price for the average farmer. Most of the land was purchased by land speculators who planned to sell it later for a profit.

The third ordinance passed by Congress was the Northwest Ordinance of 1787. In the vast open spaces of the Northwest Territory, people often just took over land with no legal rights. They were known as squatters. The government established this ordinance to stop squatters from taking land without paying for it.

The new ordinance also set up a form of government for territories before they could become states. Congress assigned each territory a governor, a secretary, and three judges. When the population of the territory reached 5,000, it could choose an assembly, a legislative body that could create laws in the territory. The assembly could send to Congress a delegate who would be a nonvoting member until the territory grew to become a state. Statehood would be achieved at 60,000 residents.

The ordinance also permanently prohibited citizens living north of the Ohio River from owning slaves. The ordinance did not free any slaves, however. Those already owned by slaveholders and held in bondage in existing states would remain slaves. Any fugitive slaves could be captured and returned to their owners in other states that accepted slavery.

Congress passed the three land ordinances in four short years. The ordinances were meant to add new territory in an orderly process. Still, the new government could barely keep up with rapid westward expansion. Taming the West and controlling new states was just one of the problems facing the young nation.

Settlers on the frontier lived under new ordinances passed by Congress.

The new government struggled under the shortcomings of the Articles of Confederation. For example, the federal government did not pay the salary and travel costs of congressmen at the time. That money had to come from the people back home, and lawmakers from poorer areas sometimes stayed away.

When Congress could not gather the minimum number of members needed to conduct business, the needs of the nation went unmet.

A TROUBLED NATION

Debt and poverty were problems throughout the country. The United States still had war debt, and many of the states had no money in their treasuries. They approved new taxes in an effort to raise funds, but struggling private citizens did not have the money to pay more taxes. The tax problem became similar to what the colonists had faced under King George.

The crisis hit farmers hard. Creditors who had lent them money to buy seeds had once accepted crops or other goods as payment. Now they expected to be paid in gold or silver because they needed the money to pay their own debt. If a farmer's crop was not successful, he could not pay. Sometimes a farmer not only lost his land but had to go to jail for failure to pay.

On August 29, 1786, a farmer named Daniel Shays led an angry group of farmers and others in an attack on the courthouse in Northampton, Massachusetts. The court was taking land away from farmers to satisfy debts they owed. The group wanted to stop the court proceedings, which they thought would allow farmers to keep their land. The attack began what was known as Shays' Rebellion.

James Bowdoin

Massachusetts Governor James Bowdoin asked Congress for help. However, there was no money to raise an army because states had refused to pay the taxes Congress had requested. The federal government offered no help. Massachusetts would have to defend itself.

Shays struck again in September, when he led 600 men to the courthouse in Springfield. Once again, they closed down the proceedings. Governor Bowdoin asked wealthy landowners for money to raise a militia, a large

Angry protesters seized control of a Massachusetts courthouse as part of the uprising known as Shays' Rebellion.

group of armed men, and a group of 4,400 militia members were sent to break up the mob.

Shays refused to stop his attacks. He led 2,000 men in another attack on Springfield late in January 1787. This time they planned to swarm the arsenal, where they could take guns and ammunition. Bowdoin again sent the militia. Shays and his men were turned back.

Shays fled into Vermont. He was a wanted man for trying to overthrow the government, but to the poor farmers of the state, he was a hero. He supported them when no one else would. Eventually, Shays and other rebels received pardons from John Hancock, the man who replaced

32

Bowdoin as governor in 1787.

Shays' Rebellion shook the country, as did unrest occurring in other states. Jonathan Smith, the delegate from Massachusetts, called it the "black cloud that rose in the east." People felt the rebellion proved the country was falling apart. Politicians and government leaders realized the states were at risk. Even during a small uprising, Congress was unable to provide military defense.

Congress wanted to pass an amendment to give itself more power. In order to amend the Articles, a unanimous vote was necessary. Some states refused to support the amendment, and it failed. Many people realized that the governing document of the country was not working. George Washington criticized the weak government structure created by the Articles of Confederation as being "little more than the shadow without the substance." The document no longer served the needs of an expanding nation.

A NEW CONSTITUTION

After the problems in Massachusetts, officials called
a Constitutional Convention in Philadelphia in May
1787 "for the sole purpose of revising the Articles of
Confederation." Once again, the delegates faced blistering
hot weather. Twelve of the 13 states were represented.
Rhode Island refused to send a delegate.

By the terms of the Articles, a unanimous vote was

George Washington presided over the 1787 Constitutional Convention.

34

needed to change the document. Technically, the men gathered in Philadelphia could not follow their charge and alter the Articles. Yet it was clear something needed to be done.

At the outset, delegates did not agree about what action to take. Some of them believed they should create a whole new constitution, although they had no order to do so. Opinions were divided between Federalists and Anti-Federalists.

Anti-Federalists were against both a new constitution and a stronger federal government. Patrick Henry was so opposed to the idea of a new constitution that he refused to take part in the convention, saying, "I smell a rat." Henry and other Anti-Federalists such as Richard Henry Lee—the man who had years earlier called for a document to unite the colonies—feared a stronger government would deprive individuals of their rights. They wanted to solve problems by amending the existing Articles of Confederation and sticking with a minimal form of federal authority.

Federalists wanted a stronger central government. George Washington and Alexander Hamilton were Federalists. They wanted to write an entirely new constitution. In this, they had the support of James Madison—a small, quiet, and thoughtful man who was Thomas Jefferson's neighbor in Virginia. Madison emerged as a leader in the push for a new constitution.

The convention continued through the long, hot Philadelphia days, until early September. Delegates worked behind closed windows and drawn drapes to maintain secrecy, and they slowly worked out their disagreements.

The issue of slavery caused heated arguments. Delegates from Northern states wanted to abolish slavery, but many whites in Southern states depended on slave labor to work their cotton and tobacco fields. Delegates from these states threatened to leave the convention if a constitution did not allow slavery. They also wanted to count slaves as part of their states' population in order to gain more representatives in the proposed House of Representatives.

36

Madison wrote early drafts of the proposed constitution, and he was determined it find acceptance. He came up with a compromise that allowed Southern states to count three-fifths of their slave population. That meant five slaves would count as three people when figuring a state's total population. Madison also got Northern delegates

James Madison

to agree that runaway slaves found in their states could be captured and sent back to their owners in the South. New slaves could be brought to America only until the year 1808. Neither side really liked the solution, but they finally agreed, in order to move forward.

After a great deal of debate, during which it appeared the very future of the United States was in doubt, Madison and other Federalists got much of what they wanted. When it seemed the constitution would never be finished, Benjamin

37

Benjamin Franklin helped convince delegates to accept a new constitution.

Franklin's support turned the tide. He said, "I consent, Sir, to this Constitution because I expect no better, and because I am not sure that it is not the best." The other delegates admired Franklin, and many of them agreed with his words.

The Constitution adopted by the delegates was very different from the Articles of Confederation. As Madison had suggested, the document divided Congress into two chambers, the House of Representatives and the Senate. Each state would have two senators, putting small states on equal footing with larger ones. In the House, each state's representation would be determined by population. States with larger populations would send more representatives to the House. The two chambers of Congress would be responsible for writing laws.

Madison's document also created two new branches of government. The first was the judiciary branch, which was given power to interpret the laws. A federal court system was put in place. One job of the judiciary would be to make sure the president and the Congress did not overstep the authority given them by the Constitution.

The executive branch was also created. With this branch, the Constitution established an individual leader for the country. The United States would have a president, who would be elected by the citizens every four years. The president would command the armed forces, manage foreign relations, and decide whether to sign or veto bills passed by Congress.

Having three branches of government created a

system of checks and balances. No individual branch could overpower the other two.

Other major differences between the Constitution and the Articles of Confederation included the power of Congress to levy taxes instead of simply requesting them. Congress also had the right to regulate trade between the states and raise an army. And unlike the Articles of Confederation, a unanimous vote was not needed to amend the Constitution. A vote consisting of two-thirds of both houses of Congress would pass an amendment, which would then be sent to the states for ratification. To pass a law, majority votes in the House and Senate were needed, along with the signature of the president.

A committee wrote the final document. While much of Madison's first draft was retained, it was a delegate named Gouverneur Morris who wrote the famous preamble. His stirring words, "We the people of the United States, in order to form a more perfect Union…" capture the spirit of American democracy. The Constitution would be the supreme law of the land.

Federalists James Madison, Alexander Hamilton, and John Jay then took action to make sure the Constitution would be ratified. They wrote and published the *Federalist Papers*, a series of 85 essays that supported the new Constitution. They published the essays in New York newspapers. Their effort was the

Gouverneur Morris

first time in history such a campaign had taken place, and it played an important part in swaying public opinion.

Thanks to the impact of the *Federalist Papers*, the Constitution was ratified in all 13 states over the course of the next two years. It went into effect in March 1789. The Articles of Confederation had guided the young country for 13 years. The document had provided a government for the United States as it battled for freedom and finally established itself as an independent nation.

41

GLOSSARY

amendment—a formal change made to a law or legal document such as the Constitution

confederation—a group that works together and shares leadership

conspiracy—a plot among a group of people to commit a crime

coup—a move to overturn a governing authority

delegates—people who represent a larger group of people at a meeting

indentured servants—people who work for a certain period of time in return for payment of travel and living costs

ordinances—decrees or laws

philosopher—a person who studies truth, wisdom, and reality

ratify—to formally approve

speculators—people who buy and sell land, taking a risk with the expectation of an increase in the value of what they own

unanimous—agreed upon by all parties

DID YOU KNOW?

- John Dickinson initially opposed breaking away from Britain and refused to sign the Declaration of Independence. As a patriot, he later supported the decision in spite of his personal opinion.

- Robert Morris and Roger Sherman were the only two men to sign the Articles of Confederation, the Declaration of Independence, and the Constitution.

- The state of Pennsylvania issued a proclamation signed by Benjamin Franklin offering a reward for the capture of Daniel Shays.

- James Madison was the president during the War of 1812 when British soldiers burned the White House. His wife, Dolley, saved an important portrait of George Washington from the fire.

IMPORTANT DATES

Timeline

1775	The Revolutionary War begins.
1776	The Second Continental Congress meets in Philadelphia; Declaration of Independence is signed and the Articles of Confederation are drafted.
1777	Congress adopts final draft of the Articles of Confederation.
1781	The Articles of Confederation are ratified; fighting in the Revolutionary War ends.
1783	The Newburgh Conspiracy fails; the Treaty of Paris is signed by the United States and Great Britain, recognizing the independence of the United States.
1786	Shays' Rebellion begins in Massachusetts.
1787	Constitutional Convention meets in Philadelphia to revise the Articles of Confederation; a new constitution is drafted.
1789	The U.S. Constitution is ratified; the Articles of Confederation no longer govern the United States.

IMPORTANT PEOPLE

JOHN DICKINSON (1732–1808)
Delegate to the Constitutional Convention and author of the Articles of Confederation

BENJAMIN FRANKLIN (1706–1790)
Scientist, popular writer, and elder statesman as a delegate at the Constitutional Convention

JAMES MADISON (1751–1836)
Father of the Constitution and fourth president of the United States

GOUVERNEUR MORRIS (1752–1816)
Pennsylvania delegate to the Continental Congress; a brilliant speaker who wrote the preamble to the Constitution

ROBERT MORRIS (1734–1806)
Superintendent of Finance for the federal government and founder of the Bank of North America; went bankrupt during George Washington's presidency and died in debtor's prison

WANT TO KNOW MORE?

At the Library

Ford, Carin T. *Thomas Jefferson: The Third President.* Berkeley Heights,
 N.J.: Enslow Publishers, 2003.

Fradin, Dennis Brindell. *Who Was Ben Franklin?* New York: Grosset &
 Dunlap, 2002.

Gaines, Ann. *James Madison.* Chanhassen, Minn.: Child's World, 2002.

Marcovitz, Hal. *The Constitution.* Philadelphia: Mason Crest
 Publishers, 2003.

On the Web

For more information on *The Articles of Confederation*, use FactHound
to track down Web sites related to this book.

1. Go to *www.facthound.com*

2. Type in a search word related to this book
 or this book ID: 0756516277

3. Click on the *Fetch It* button.

Your trusty FactHound will fetch the best Web sites for you!

On the Road

Independence Hall

Independence Visitor Center

One North Independence Mall West

Sixth and Market Streets

Philadelphia, PA 19106

215/925-6101

The place where the Articles of
Confederation were debated and
approved

Montpelier

11407 Constitution Highway

Montpelier Station, VA 22957

540/672-2728

The home of James Madison, the
author of the Constitution and
fourth president of the United States

Look for more We the People books about this era:

The Battles of Lexington and Concord
ISBN 0-7565-0490-2

The Bill of Rights
ISBN 0-7565-0151-2

The Boston Massacre
ISBN 0-7565-0832-0

The Boston Tea Party
ISBN 0-7565-0040-0

The Declaration of Independence
ISBN 0-7565-0042-7

*Great Women of the American
Revolution*
ISBN 0-7565-0838-X

The Minutemen
ISBN 0-7565-0842-8

Monticello
ISBN 0-7565-0491-0

Mount Vernon
ISBN 0-7565-0682-4

Paul Revere's Ride
ISBN 0-7565-0492-9

The U.S. Constitution
ISBN 0-7565-0493-7

Valley Forge
ISBN 0-7565-0615-8

A complete list of We the People titles is available on our Web site:
www.compasspointbooks.com

47

INDEX

About the Author
Renée C. Rebman lives in Lexington, Ohio. She has written several nonfiction books for children and particularly enjoys historical subjects. She is also a published playwright. Her plays are produced in schools and community theaters across the country.